How to ace your Spanish oral

Questions and answers on all topics

With English Translation and glossary

This book is dedicated to my father David, who inspired my love of languages.

TABLE OF CONTENTS

Introduction   4

Introducing yourself in Spanish   6

Including age, appearance and character of family members

House, home and daily routine   8

Including friend and family outings, ideal family, marriage and relationships

Town and region   14

Including weather and climate, transport, tourists and young people

Holidays   19

Including past and future holidays, ideal holiday, purpose of holidays

Festivals and Christmas   22

Including past and future Christmases

Education and work   23

Including past, present and future education and employment

Modern world and environment   29

Including world problems and solutions, poverty, technology, mobile phones, internet

Social activities, fitness and health   40

Including hobbies, TV, books, cinema, sport, food and drink, smoking, drugs, alcohol

Glossary of impressive phrases   47

Introduction

In my ten years of teaching French and Spanish, I have helped hundreds of students get top marks in their oral exams. One of those students was Maddy O'Neil, who achieved top marks at GCSE, AS and A level and has gone one to study Spanish at Bristol university. It has been a delight working with Maddy, and I believe all my readers will derive even more benefit from this teacher / student collaborative approach.

In this book we have produced a full set of answers to the GCSE oral questions, together with an English translation and glossary of key phrases. One size does not fit all, and you may wish to cut and paste, pick and choose which answers or phrases you include in your own work. You may need to change the description of your family, town and school in order to be factually correct but the overall structures and expressions can still be included.

It's not cheating!

Languages are hard to learn in a classroom, and teachers rarely have enough time to give each student the one-to-one time they need for oral practice. There are plenty of students out there getting help outside school, and here's your chance to be one of them, at a fraction of the cost.

Children learn by hearing and copying, and that's what is happening here. Once those phrases are stuck in your head, you'll be able to use them not only in the oral exam but in the writing paper and out and about in real life. To make the most of the learning experience, test yourself by looking at the English and translating it into Spanish, then checking with the Spanish text.

There is a fair bit of repetition, and obviously on the day you shouldn't repeat the Spanish for "I'm lucky because" at the beginning of every answer, but I have put them in wherever possible, to show you what *is* possible, and also because you will only be asked a handful of questions, so you need to make the most of the chance to show off.

There is a positive thread running throughout the answers. If you use them word for word you will end up sounding like a super-hardworking clean-living sports enthusiast with a strong environmental awareness and an abundance of energy. Even if this isn't you, pretending that it is will give you a chance to use some great Spanish idioms. Girls will need to make a few adjustments, as the viewpoint is mainly male so adjectives are masculine and based on the male subject.

I have highlighted the structures and expressions examiners will be looking out for, so you'll see how it's possible to change a boring sentence like "I live in London" earning you no points at all, to something much more eye-catching like "I'm lucky because I've been living in London for 5 years and it's the best city in the world." Rather than just "I like swimming" you can say "I am lucky because there is a pool near my house and I usually go there (suelo) every day so that I can keep fit. This way you are using back to back impressive phrases.

All these highlighted structures are listed in the glossary, so test yourself on the glossary pages to get an intensive immersion experience in the top phrases.

As I tell my students, the oral and the writing is your chance to be in the driving seat. So fire these highlighted expressions at the examiner like a machine gun, not just in the oral, but in your writing as well, and you'll be well on the way to top marks. So what are you waiting for? Go knock 'em dead!

INTRODUCING YOURSELF

About you

Me llamo .... y tengo ..... años. Soy bastante grande, tengo los ojos azules y el pelo rubio. Soy muy divertido, deportista e inteligente, pero a veces un poco perezoso, sobre todo cuando por la mañana cuando no tengo ganas de ir al colegio y tengo que pegarme un madrugón.

My name is .... and I'm ..... years old. I am quite tall, I have blonde hair and blue eyes. I am very funny, sporty, and intelligent but sometimes a bit lazy, especially in the mornings when I don't want to go to school.

About your interests and hobbies

Cuando tengo tiempo / una vez a la semana / todos los días / el sábado, me gusta hacer ciclismo con mi padre y los fines de semana suelo jugar al tenis con mi amigo en el parque porque es mi deporte favorito y soy adicto. Tengo suerte porque soy miembro de un club de tenis desde hace dos años. Paso mucho tiempo viendo la televisión, aunque sea malo para la salud, para relajarme y olvidar el estrés del colegio. Tengo ganas de aprender el ajedrez porque me parece más interesante que ver la tele.

When I have time / once a week / every day / on Saturdays, I like to go cycling with my father and at the weekends I usually play tennis with my friend in the park because it's my favourite sport and I'm addicted to it. I'm lucky because I have been a member of a tennis club for 2 years. I spend a lot of time watching TV, although it is bad for your health, in order to relax and to forget the stress of school. I'd like to learn chess because it seems more interesting than watching TV.

Your family

En mi familia hay cinco personas, mi madre, mi padre, mis dos hermanos y yo. Mi hermano mayor es grande, delgado, muy guapo y más deportista que yo. Tiene el pelo marrón y los ojos verdes. Le gusta jugar al futbol y hacer la natación. Mi hermano menor tiene el pelo rubio y los ojos azules. Siempre hace el tonto. Nos parecemos mucho y nos llevamos bien pero cuando tiene un humor de perros, es harina de otro costal. Me llevo bastante bien con mis padres, pero a veces discutimos, porque no les gusta cuando vuelvo tarde a casa.

In my family there are 5 people: my mother, my father, my two brothers and me. My older brother is tall, slim, very handsome and sportier than me. He has brown hair and green eyes.

He is always messing about. He likes playing football and going swimming. My younger brother has blond hair and blue eyes. We look very similar and we get on well, but when he's in a bad mood that's another matter entirely. I get on quite well with my parents, but sometimes we argue because they don't like it when I come home late.

HOUSE, HOME AND DAILY ROUTINE

Your house

Tengo suerte porque es la mejor casa del mundo y vivo allí desde hace cinco años. Mi casa es grande, moderna y cómoda. En la planta baja hay la cocina, el salón, el despacho y el comedor. En el primer piso hay cuatro dormitorios y un cuarto de baño. Detrás de la casa hay un gran jardín donde se puede jugar al futbol cuando hace buen tiempo. Lo que más me gusta es que ya no tengo que compartir mi dormitorio con mi hermano porque es tan molesto. Lo que no me gusta es el ruido del tráfico.

I am lucky because it is the best house in the world and I have been living there for 5 years. My house is big, modern and comfortable. On the ground floor there is the kitchen, the lounge, the office and the dining room. On the first floor there are four bedrooms and a bathroom. Behind the house is a big garden where you can play football when it is good weather. What I like most is that I no longer have to share my bedroom with my brother because he is so annoying. What I don't like is the traffic noise.

Your bedroom

Mi dormitorio está en el primer piso al lado del dormitorio de mis padres. Al lado de la cama hay un armario y delante de la ventana hay un escritorio donde hago mis deberes. Las paredes son azules porque es mi color favorito, y tengo suerte porque tengo no solo un ordenador portátil sino también una televisión, así que puedo fácilmente pasar muchísimas horas relajándome sin tener que bajar la escalera.

My bedroom is on the first floor by my parents' bedroom. Next to the bed there is a cupboard and in front of the window is a desk where I do my homework. The walls are blue because it's my favourite colour and I'm lucky because I not only have a laptop but also a television so I can easily spend many hours relaxing without having to go downstairs.

Ideal house

Si fuera rico me compraría mi casa ideal. Mi casa ideal sería enorme, moderna y cómoda, con una gran piscina para que pueda hacer natación todos los días. Si fuera riquísima, habría también un cine donde pasaría muchísimas horas viendo películas con mis amigos, y un jardín con árboles y flores. Estaría cerca del centro de Londres para que mis amigos puedan visitarme.

If I were rich I would buy my ideal house. My ideal house would be enormous, modern and comfortable with a big pool so I could swim every day. If I was really rich there would also be a cinema where I would spend many hours watching films with my friends, and a garden with trees and flowers. It would be near the centre of London so that my friends could visit me.

What is the ideal family?

No creo que haya la familia ideal – es que el niño necesita amor la estabilidad, y el tipo de familia no importa. Lo importante es que puedas contar con tu familia. Hoy en día hay un montón de tipos de familia – con parejas homosexuales, familias monoparentales y tradicionales, familias numerosas, hijos únicos, y todos tienen su valor. Tengo suerte porque en mi familia nos llevamos bien.

I don't think there is such a thing as the ideal family – just that a child needs love and stability and the type of family doesn't matter. The important thing is to be able to rely on your family. Nowadays there are loads of different types of family – with homosexual couples, single parents, traditional families, large families and only children, and all have their value.

Is marriage important?

No importa si estás casado o no, sobre todo porque tantos matrimonios fracasan, y el número de personas solteras crece. Muchos niños son testigos de divorcio y viven con hermanastros y hermanastras. No sé si voy a casarme o no. Me gustaría vivir con alguien durante unos años antes de tomar una decisión tan importante. Deberíamos aprender más sobre las relaciones en el colegio para que sepamos lo que supone el matrimonio.

It doesn't matter if you are married or not, especially because so many marriages break down and the number of single people is increasing. I don't know if I will get married or not. I'd like to live with someone for a few years before making such an important decision. We should learn more about relationships at school so that we know what marriage involves.

Describe your best friend

Tengo suerte porque tengo el mejor amigo del mundo que se llama …… Somos amigos desde hace diez años. Tiene los ojos azules y el pelo rubio. Es más grande que yo, pero menos deportista. Nos llevamos bien porque tenemos muchos pasatiempos en común – nos gustan los videojuegos e solemos ir de compras juntos todos los fines de semana.

Además, tenemos lo mismo sentido de humor. ¡Qué suerte! Lo único es que no le gusta el futbol y yo soy fanático del Manchester United. Si le gustara el futbol seria perfecto.

I am lucky because I have the best friend in the world called .... We have been friends for ten years. He has blue eyes and blonde hair. He is taller than me, but less sporty. We get on well because we have lots of hobbies in common – we like videogames and we usually go shopping together at the weekend. Also we have the same sense of humour. How lucky! The only thing is that he doesn't like football and I'm a Man United fan. If he liked football he would be perfect.

Recent outing with best friend

El fin de semana pasado fui con .... a Londres para ir de compras. Tuve que comprar un regalo para mi madre para su cumpleaños. Al llegar al centro, compramos muchísima ropa, y después comimos en una pizzería. ¡Qué deliciosa! Lo malo fue que casi olvidé de comprar un regalo para mi madre. Por suerte hay una tienda cerca de mi casa donde se vende libros interesantes sobre la naturaleza. Escoge un libro, lo compré y volví a casa. A mi madre le gustó muchísimo.

Last weekend I went with .... to London to go shopping. I had to buy a presents for my mother for her birthday. On arriving in the centre, we bought a lot of clothes and afterwards we ate lunch in a pizzeria. How delicious! The bad thing was that I almost forgot to buy a present for my mother. Luckily there is a shop near my house where they sell interesting books on nature. I chose a book, bought it and went home. My mother really loved it.

Future outing with best friend

El fin de semana que viene, vamos a ir de compras para buscar nueva ropa. Después iremos al cine para ver la nueva película de James Bond porque nos encantan las películas de acción. Antes de volver a casa cenaremos en un restaurante con nos compañeros de clase y discutiremos la película.

Next weekend we are going to go shopping to look for new clothes. Afterwards we will go to the cinema to see the new Bond film because we love action films. Before going home, we will have dinner in a restaurant with our school friends and we will discuss the film.

Daily routine

Normalmente, por la mañana me pego un madrugón porque tengo que ir al colegio. Me despierto a las siete, me levanto, me ducho y me visto antes de desayunar. Voy al colegio en autobús a las ocho y al llegar, charlo con mis amigos. Las clases empiezan a las nueve y tenemos ocho clases de cuarenta minutos al día. Vuelvo a casa a las cuatro y media, hago mis deberes, ceno con mi familia y después de cenar, suelo ver la tele en el salón o chatear por internet con mis amigos. Me acuesto sobre las diez.

Normally in the morning I have to get up really early because I have to go to school. I wake up at 7, I get up, shower and get dressed before having breakfast. I go to school by bus at 8 and when I arrive I chat to my friends. Lessons begin at 9 and we have 8 lessons of 40 minutes each per day. I go home at 4.30, do my homework, eat with my family and after eating I usually watch TV in the lounge or chat online with my friends. I go to bed around 10.

Daily routine weekend

El fin de semana, suelo levantarme más tarde que normalmente porque no tengo que ir al colegio. Desayuno sobre las once y salgo con mis amigos al parque o al centro comercial para ir de compras. Por la tarde suelo jugar al tenis en el polideportivo, y siempre cenamos juntos en familia. A veces vemos una película en Netflix o pasamos la tarde jugando a las cartas. Paso unas horas haciendo mis deberes, pero suelo dejarlos para el final.

At the weekend I get up later than usual because I don't have to go to school. I have breakfast around 11 and I go out with my friends to the park or the shopping mall to go shopping. In the afternoon I usually play tennis at the sports centre, and we always have dinner together as a family. Sometimes we watch a film on Netflix or we spend the evening playing cards. I spend a few hours doing my homework but I usually leave it until the last minute.

This morning

Hoy me pegué un madrugón porque tuve que ir al colegio, me duché, me vestí y desayuné de prisa antes de irme. Siempre tengo prisa por la mañana. Fui al colegio en autobús y llegué a las ocho. Al llegar, charlé con mis amigos e hice un poco más revisión para mi examen oral de español.

Today I got up really early because I had to go to school, I showered, got dressed and had breakfast quickly before leaving. I am always in a hurry in the morning. I went to school by bus and arrived at 8. I chatted with my friends and did a bit more revision for my Spanish oral exam.

This evening

Al llegar a casa voy a relajarme antes de hacer mis deberes. Veré la tele e intentaré olvidar el estrés del día escolar. ¡Ojalá pudiera! Cenaré sobre las siete. Después charlaré con mis compañeros de clase en las redes sociales, porque soy adicto y no puedo prescindir de Facebook y Snapchat.

When I get home I'm going to relax before doing my homework. I will watch TV and I will try to forget the stress of the school day. If only I could! I will have dinner around 7. Afterwards I will chat with my school friends on social networks because I am addicted and I can't manage without Facebook and Snapchat.

What you would change about your routine

Si fuera posible, no haría deberes durante la semana. Cada tarde tengo que hacer dos horas de deberes y estoy siempre cansado y estresado. Además, me gustaría quedarme acostado hasta más tarde. Los científicos dicen que los jóvenes necesitan más sueño y estoy completamente de acuerdo. El colegio debería empezar al mediodía.

If it were possible, I wouldn't do homework during the week. Every evening I have to do two hours of homework and I am always tired and stressed. Also I would like to stay in bed until later. Scientists say that young people need more sleep and I am completely in agreement. School should start at midday.

Helping at home

Para ayudar mis padres lavo los platos / el coche, arreglo mi dormitorio, paso la aspiradora, pongo / quito la mesa, preparo la comida y a veces limpio la cocina. No obstante, me cuesta hacerlo ahora porque los profes nos dan tantos deberes y paso mucho tiempo revisando para mis exámenes. SI tuviera menos deberes, haría más para ayudar.

To help my parents I wash the dishes / the car, I tidy my room, I hoover, I lay / clear the table, I cook meals and sometimes I clean the kitchen. However, I struggle to do it now because the teachers give us so much homework and I spend a lot of time revising for exams. If I had less homework I would do more to help.

Help at home yesterday

Ayer lavé los platos, puse la mesa y arreglé mi dormitorio. Habría hecho más si hubiera tenido el tiempo, pero los profes nos dan demasiados deberes.

Yesterday I washed the dishes, laid the table and tidied my room. I would have done more if I had had time, but the teachers give us too much homework.

Cooking at home

Por lo general, mi madre prepara la comida, pero cuando no está, lo hago yo. Me gusta cocinar, y si tuviera el tiempo haría más, pero los profes nos dan demasiados deberes.

In general, my mother cooks the meals, but when she's not there, I do it. I like cooking, and if I had the time I would do more, but the teachers give us too much homework.

Plans for next weekend with family

El fin de semana que viene, me gustaría hacer ciclismo con mi padre porque nos gusta pasar tiempo al aire libre. Por la tarde voy a ir de compras con mi madre. Después iremos al cine para ver la nueva película de James Bond porque nos encantan las películas de acción. Antes de volver a casa cenaremos en un restaurante y discutiremos la película. Al llegar a casa me acostaré y dormiré como un tronco.

Next weekend I'd like to go cycling with my dad because we like spending time in the fresh air. In the afternoon I'm going to go shopping with my mother. Afterwards we will go to the cinema to see the new Bond film because we love action films. Before going home, we will have dinner in a restaurant and discuss the film. When I get home I will go to bed and sleep like a log.

Recent family activity

El fin de semana pasado fuimos al parque para pasear al perro, fuimos de compras y después volvimos a casa para comer. Por la tarde fuimos a visitar a mis abuelos que viven cerca de nosotros, tomamos té y comimos pasteles deliciosos. Al volver decidimos ver una película de acción. Me acosté a las once y dormí como un tronco.

Last weekend we went to the park to walk the dog, we went shopping and then we went home to eat. In the afternoon we went to visit my grandparents who live near us, we had tea and ate delicious cakes. When we got back (on returning) we decided to watch an action film. I went to bed at 11 and slept like a log.

TOWN AND REGIOIN

Describe your town

Tengo suerte porque vivo en Londres desde hace diez años y es la mejor ciudad del mundo. Lo que más me gusta es que hay un montón de cosas que hacer. Se puede ir al cine, al teatro, a restaurantes, a museos, y hay tiendas, polideportivos y parques donde se puede jugar al tenis o al futbol. Suelo ir al cine todos los fines de semana porque me encantan las películas. Lo que no me gusta es que hay mucho tráfico.

I'm lucky because I've been living in London for ten years and it's the best city in the world. What I like most is that there is a lot to do. You can go to the cinema, to the theatre, to restaurants, to museums, and there are shops, sports centres, parks where you can play tennis or football. I usually go to the cinema every weekend because I love films.

Recent outing in town

El fin de semana pasado fui con .... a Londres para ir de compras. Tuve que comprar un regalo para mi madre para su cumpleaños. Al llegar al centro, compramos muchísima ropa, y después comimos en una pizzería. ¡Qué deliciosa! Lo malo fue que casi olvidé de comprar un regalo para mi madre. Por suerte hay una tienda cerca de mi casa donde se vende libros interesantes sobre la naturaleza. Escoge un libro, lo compré y volví a casa. Le regalé el libro y a mi madre le gustó muchísimo.

Last weekend I went with .... to London to go shopping. I had to buy a presents for my mother for her birthday. On arriving in the centre, we bought a lot of clothes and afterwards we ate lunch in a pizzeria. How delicious! The bad thing was that I almost forgot to buy a present for my mother. Luckily there is a shop near my house where they sell interesting books on nature. I chose a book, bought it and went home. I gave her the book and my mother really loved it.

What is there for young people in your town?

nucho que hacer para los jóvenes en mi barrio. Hay un
ede hacer deporte y muchas distracciones divertidas. Suelo ir al
al tenis en el parque. Lo malo es que todo eso cuesta un ojo de
melo. Sería perfecto si hubiera un lugar para los jóvenes donde
uvenil. Podríamos divertirnos sin gastarse un riñón.

13

I'm lucky because there is a lot to do for young people in my area. There is a sports centre where you can do sport and lots of fun activities. I usually go to the cinema, go shopping or play tennis in the park. The bad thing is that all this costs an arm and a leg and I can't afford it. It would be perfect if there was a place where young people could get together like a youth club. We could have fun without it costing a fortune.

What is there for tourists in your town?

No hay muchos sitios turísticos en mi barrio, pero tenemos suerte porque se puede fácilmente ir a Londres en tren para ver los monumentos, los museos y las galerías de arte. También se puede visitar el palacio de Buckingham donde vive la reina de Inglaterra. Si pudiera, visitaría los sitios turísticos más a menudo, pero cuesta un ojo de la cara y no puedo permitírmelo.

There aren't many tourist attractions in my area but we are lucky because you can easily go to London by train to see the sights, the museums and art galleries. You can also visit Buckingham Palace where the Queen of England lives.

What would you do for young people in your town?

Lo que más me preocupa es que las actividades en mi barrio cuestan un ojo de la cara. Si pudiera cambiar algo en mi barrio, construiría un centro juvenil para que los jóvenes puedan reunirse y divertirse sin gastarse un riñón. Además, pondría más rutas para ciclistas porque me encanta el ciclismo y las carreteras son demasiadas peligrosas para ciclistas debido al tráfico.

What worries me most is that the activities in my area cost a fortune. If I could change something in my area, I would build a youth centre so that young people could meet up and have fun without having to pay through the nose for it. Also, I would put in more cycle paths because I love cycling and the roads are too dangerous for cyclists due to the traffic.

Town and countryside

En mi opinión, la ciudad es mejor que el campo por muchas razones. Por ejemplo, se puede comer en restaurantes, ver películas, ir de compras y reunirse con amigos. Sobre todo, lo que más me gusta es el transporte público, porque no conduzco y tengo que coger el autobús para ir a ver a mis amigos. Si viviera en el campo, no podría ver mis amigos tan fácilmente. Sin embargo, hay ventajas de vivir en el campo. Es más tranquilo que la ciudad, es más relajante y se puede pasear al aire libre. En la ciudad, lo que más me preocupa es el tráfico y la contaminación del aire que van empeorando.

In my opinion the city is better than the countryside for many reasons. For example, you can eat in restaurants, watch films, go shopping and meet up with friends. What I like most is the public transport because I don't drive and I have to take the bus to go and see my friends. If I lived in the countryside I wouldn't be able to see my friends so easily. However, there are advantages of living in the countryside. It is quieter than the city, it's more relaxing and you can walk in the fresh air. In the city the traffic and air pollution which are getting worse.

Where will you live in the future?

Cuando sea mayor, me gustaría seguir viviendo en Londres para que pueda aprovechar todas las actividades y quedarme cerca de mis amigos. Viviré en una casa moderna y grande, bien equipado, con vistas bonitas. Es importante que haya suficiente espacio para dar fiestas porque me encanta bailar.

When I'm older I would like to continue living in London so I can make the most of all the activities and stay close to my friends. I will live in a modern, large, well-appointed house with pretty views. It is important that there is enough space to have parties because I love dancing.

Weather in your region today

Hoy hace buen tiempo, pero es posible que más tarde llueva a mares. Vamos a ver.

Today the weather is good but it might pour with rain later. We shall see.

Seasonal changes in your region

En invierno hace más frio que en verano, pero el clima está cambiando, y ya no nieva en invierno como antes. La diferencia entre las estaciones está disminuyendo debido al calentamiento global.

In winter it is colder than in summer, but the climate is changing and it no longer snows in winter as it used to. The difference between the seasons is diminishing due to global warming.

Climate comparison with Spain

En España hace más calor que en Inglaterra, y por eso a los ingleses les encanta pasar las vacaciones allí. No obstante, en verano el calor puede ser insoportable. Aquí no hay tantas diferencias de clima durante el año. Llueve a mares todo el año.

In Spain it is hotter than in England and therefore the English love spending the holidays there. However, in summer the heat can be unbearable. Here there aren't such differences in weather during the year. It pours with rain all year round.

Climate change in your region

El clima va cambiando / está cambiando – no hay duda. Los coches y los aviones emiten gases tóxicos que suben a la atmosfera y causan el calentamiento global y el efecto invernadero. Los mares suben y hay islas que empiezan a desaparecer. Hay más inundaciones y más tormentas que antes. Tenemos que actuar antes de que sea demasiado tarde para salvar el planeta.

The climate is changing – there's no doubt about it. Cars and planes emit toxic gases which go up into the atmosphere and cause global warming and the greenhouse effect. The sea levels are rising and there are islands which are beginning to disappear. There are more floods and more storms than before. We need to act before it's too late to save the planet.

Climate change solution

Tenemos que actuar lo antes posible para salvar el planeta. Tenemos que usar la bici en lugar del coche, viajar menos en avión y ahorrar energía para que los recursos naturales no se agoten. Deberíamos parar la destrucción de las selvas tropicales que producen el oxígeno que necesitamos. Deberíamos dejar de comer tanta carne porque las vacas (tanto como) los coches emiten gases tóxicos que causan el cambio climático.

We need to act as soon as possible to save the planet. We need to use bikes instead of the car, travel less by plane and save energy so that natural resources don't run out. We should stop the destruction of tropical forests which produce the oxygen we need. We should stop eating so much meat because the cows, just like the cars, give off toxic gases which cause climate change.

Transport in your region

Tengo suerte porque hay una buena red de transporte en mi barrio. Hay trenes, autobuses y el metro y se puede fácilmente desplazarse. Lo único es que las calles son ruidosas y hay demasiados atascos. Si hubiera más rutas para ciclistas pienso que no habría tanta contaminación del aire.

I'm lucky because there is a good public transport network in my area. There are trains, buses and the underground and you can get around easily. The only thing is that the streets are noisy and there are too many traffic jams. If there were more cycle paths I think there wouldn't be so much air pollution.

Favourite transport

Mi transporte favorito es el avión, aunque sea malo para el medioambiente, porque es rápido, cómodo y se puede ver películas, comer, beber y leer durante el viaje. No me gusta el tren porque nunca encuentro un asiento. ¡Qué molesto!

My favourite transport is the plane, although it is bad for the environment, because it's fast, comfortable and you can watch films, eat, drink and read during the journey. I don't like trains because I never find a seat. How annoying!

HOLIDAYS

Usual holidays

Tengo suerte porque todos los años suelo ir a España en avión con mi familia y nos alojamos en un hotel cerca de la playa durante dos semanas. Me encanta porque en mi opinión es el mejor país del mundo. Hace calor, la gente es simpática y la comida riquísima. Suelo pasar muchas horas relajándome y olvidando el estrés de mi vida. Juego al tenis todos los días, tomo el sol, nado en el mar y hago nuevos amigos. Me lo paso bomba.

I'm lucky because every year I go to Spain by plane with my family and we stay in a hotel near the beach for two weeks. I love it because in my opinion it is the best country in the world. It's hot, the people are nice and the food is delicious. I usually spend hours relaxing and forgetting the stress of my life. I play tennis every day, I sunbathe, swim in the sea and make new friends. I have a great time.

Last year's holiday

Tengo suerte porque hace un año, fui a .... en ...barco / coche / avión con ...una amiga / unas amigas / un amigo / unos amigos / mi familia. Pasé .... días / semanas / meses relajándome. Nos alojamos en un hotel cerca de la playa. Tomé el sol, hice la equitación, jugué al tenis, nadé en el mar, visité monumentos históricos, descansé, leí libros, conocí a nueva gente, dormí mucho. Hice sol todos los días. Fue fenomenal. ¡Me lo pasé bomba!

I am lucky because a year ago I went to ....by boat / car / plane with a friend / with friends / with my family. I spent .... days / weeks / months relaxing. We stayed in a hotel near the beach. I sunbathed, went horseriding, played tennis, swam in the sea, visited historical sites, relaxed, read books, met new people, slept a lot. It was sunny every day. It was amazing. I had a great time.

Purchases on hoilday

Para mi mejor amigo compré una camiseta roja para su cumpleaños. Si hubiera podido, le habría comprado algo más interesante pero no podía permitírmelo.

I bought a red T-shirt for my best friend's birthday. If I could have I would have bought him something more interesting but I couldn't afford it.

Future holiday

El año que viene / cuando haya terminado mis exámenes, iré a Grecia con mi familia y unos amigos. Nos alojaremos en un hotel cerca de la playa y vamos a jugar al tenis todos los días. Tomaré el sol, nadaré en el mar y descansaré porque tendré que relajarme después de los exámenes. Espero con ganas las vacaciones.

Next year / when I have finished my exams, I will go to Greece with my family and some friends. We will stay in a hotel near the beach and we are going to play tennis every day. I will sunbathe, swim in the sea and relax because I will need to rest after the exams. I am looking forward to it.

Ideal holiday

Si fuera rica iría a Francia. Tengo ganas de ir el año que viene con mi mejor amiga para unas semanas. Nos alojaríamos en un hotel de cinco estrellas cerca de la playa. Pasaríamos todos los días relajándonos, jugando al tenis, nadando en el mar y tomando el sol. Haríamos nuevos amigos, probaríamos los platos típicos de la región y compraríamos recuerdos. Haría sol todos los días. ¡Qué perfecto!

If I was rich I would go to France. I would like to go next year with my best friend for a few weeks. We would stay in a five-star hotel near the beach. We would spend every day relaxing, playing tennis, swimming in the sea and sunbathing. We would make new friends, we would try the local dishes and buy souvenirs. It would be sunny every day. How perfect!

Holidays with parents or friends?

Lo bueno de ir de vacaciones con mis padres es que pagan todo y no tengo que pensar en nada. Nos alojamos en hoteles lujosos y comimos los platos típicos de la región. Lo malo es que tengo que visitar sitios turísticos que no me interesan. ¡Qué aburrido! Tengo ganas de ir de vacaciones con mis amigos para que pueda aprovechar la libertad y la falta de museos.

The good thing about going on holiday with my parents is that they pay for everything and I don't have to think about anything. We stay in luxury hotels and we eat local food. The bad thing is that I have to visit tourist sites which don't interest me. How boring! I would like to go on holiday with my friends so that I can make the most of the freedom and the lack of museums.

Importance of holidays

Las vacaciones son importantes por muchas razones. Primero tenemos que relajarnos después del trabajo cuando hemos currado un montón. También es importante conocer la cultura de los países extranjeros para que podamos tener un mejor entendimiento sobre la gente del mundo. Además, se puede aprovechar la oportunidad de aprender nuevos deportes y probar nuevas actividades por primera vez.

Holidays are important for many reasons. Firstly, we need to relax after work when we have been working our socks off. Also it's important to get to know the culture of foreign countries so that we can have a better understanding of the people of the world. Also, you can learn new sports and take the opportunity to try new activities for the first time.

Camping

No me gusta hacer camping porque no es cómodo. Prefiero dormir en una cama cómoda.

I don't like camping because it's not comfortable. I prefer to sleep in a comfortable bed.

FESTIVALS AND CHRISTMAS

Festivals in England

No hay muchas fiestas in Inglaterra. La única fiesta que celebramos en nuestra familia es la Navidad, mientras que en España hay un montón de fiestas durante todo el año. La mayoría son religiosas, pero también hay fiestas divertidas como la Tomatina cerca de Valencia, donde los participantes se arrojan tomates los unos a los otros. Si solo tuviéramos batallas de tomates aquí en Inglaterra. Claro que tenemos fiestas de arte y de música como en todos los países. No obstante, las fiestas de música cuestan un ojo de la cara.

There aren't many festivals in England. The only festival we celebrate in our family is Christmas, whereas in Spain there are loads of festivals all year round. Most of them are religious but there are also fun festivals like the Tomatina near Valencia where they throw tomatoes at each other. If only we had tomato battles here in England... Of course we have art and music festivals as all countries do. Music festivals cost a fortune however.

Last Christmas

El año pasado, mis abuelos vinieron a vernos y pasamos el día juntos, comiendo, bebiendo, hablando y jugando. Recibí un montón de regalos. ¡Qué bueno! Después de una comida riquísima vimos la televisión y mi abuelo se durmió en el sofá. Antes de acostarnos jugamos a las cartas, pero mi padre tocó el piano y tuvimos que taparnos los oídos.

Last year my grandparents came to see us and we spent the day together, eating, drinking, talking and playing. I received loads of presents. How great! After a delicious meal we watched television and my grandfather fell asleep on the sofa. Before going to bed we played cards but my father played the piano and we had to block our ears.

Next Christmas

Este año mis abuelos van a venir a vernos, y pasaremos el día juntos, comiendo, bebiendo, hablando y jugando. Recibiré un montón de regalos. ¡Qué bueno! Después de una comida riquísima veremos la televisión y mi abuelo se dormirá en el sofá. Antes de acostarnos jugaremos a las cartas, mi padre tocará el piano y tendremos que taparnos los oídos.

Next year my grandparents will come to see us and we will spend the day together, eating, drinking, talking and playing. I will get loads of presents. How great! After a delicious meal we will watch television and my grandfather will fall asleep on the sofa. Before going to bed we will play cards, my father will play the piano and we will have to block our ears.

EDUCATION AND WORK

Describe your school

Mi colegio se llama .... y está en .... cerca de .... Tengo suerte porque es el mejor colegio del mundo y voy allí desde hace cinco años. Lo que más me gusta es que es grande, con partes antiguas y partes modernas. Hay aulas, laboratorios, un comedor y un campo deportivo donde se puede jugar al futbol, pero no hay piscina. Si hubiera una piscine y un cine, sería perfecto.

My school is called .... and it is in .... near .... I'm lucky because it's the best school in the world and I've been going there for 5 years. What I like most is that it's big with some old parts and some modern parts. There are classrooms, laboratories, a dining room and a sports field but there isn't a pool. If there was a pool and a cinema it would be perfect.

Likes and dislikes about school

Me gusta mi colegio porque tengo muchos amigos, pero lo que no me gusta es que los profes nos dan demasiados deberes. También, si hubiera una piscina / un cine, estaría contentísimo. Si pudiera cambiar algo, cambiaría el uniforme porque es incómodo y feo. Estoy harto de él.

I like my school because I have lots of friends but what I don't like is that the teachers give us too much homework. Also if there was a pool / a cinema I would be very happy. If I could change something I would change the uniform because it's uncomfortable and ugly. I'm sick of it.

School day

Las clases empiezan a las nueve y terminan a las cuatro. Tenemos seis clases al día y cada clase dura una hora. Durante el recreo, juego con mis amigos y como un bocadillo. A menudo voy a un club durante la hora de comer. A veces voy al colegio andando, pero normalmente voy en coche y vuelvo en tren. Suelo hacer dos horas de deberes por la tarde.

Lessons begin at 9 and finish at 4. We have 6 lessons a day and each one lasts an hour. During break time I play with my friends and eat a sandwich. I often go to a club at lunchtime. Sometimes I walk to school but normally I go to school by car and come back by train. I usually do two hours of homework in the evening.

Subjects

Estoy estudiando el francés, el español, el dibujo, el latín, el inglés, el deporte, las ciencias, las matemáticas, la música, la historia y la geografía. Mi asignatura favorita es ……….porque el profe es simpático y saco buenas notas. No me gusta el latín porque es difícil, el profe es aburrido y el profe nos da demasiados deberes.

I am studying French, Spanish, art, Latin, English, sport, sciences, maths, music, history and geography. My favourite subject is ….. because the teacher is nice and I get good marks. I don't like Latin because it's difficult, the teacher is boring and the teacher gives us too much homework.

Describe a teacher

Mi profe de español es mi profe favorito por supuesto. Se llama ……………… y tiene el pelo rubio y los ojos azules. Lo que más me gusta es que es el profe más inteligente del colegio, me hace reír y al mismo tiempo siempre explica todo muy lentamente para que pueda comprender lo que hacemos.

My Spanish teacher is my favourite teacher of course. He / she is called …………. and he / she has blonde hair and blue eyes. What I like most is that he / she is the most intelligent teacher in the school, makes me laugh and at the same time always explains everything very slowly so I can understand what we are doing.

Describe your uniform

Tenemos que llevar un uniforme: [una falda negra, una camisa blanca, pantalones negros, una chaqueta negra, zapatos negros, calcetines o medias, una corbata y un jersey]. Si pudiera cambiar algo, cambiaría el uniforme porque es incómodo y feo. Estoy harto de él.

We have to wear a uniform – [a black skirt, a white shirt, black trousers, a black jacket, black shoes, socks or tights, a tie and a jumper]. If I could change something I would change the uniform because it's uncomfortable and ugly. I'm sick of it.

Opinion of uniform

Claro que hay ventajas de llevar un uniforme. No tienes que pensar en lo que vas a poner por la mañana y no hay presión de vestirse de manera elegante, de moda. Todos se parecen y así se puede evitar el acoso escolar. No obstante, en mi colegio, si pudiera cambiar algo, cambiaría el uniforme porque es incómodo y feo. Estoy harto de él.

Of course there are advantages to wearing a uniform. You don't have to think about what you are going to wear in the morning and there is no pressure to dress in a fashionable way. Everyone looks the same and in this way you can avoid bulling in schools. If I could change something I would change the uniform because it's uncomfortable and ugly. I'm sick of it.

Yesterday at school

Ayer fui al cole en autobús y al llegar, charlé con mis amigos. Las clases empezaron a las nueve y tuve cinco clases de cuarenta minutos antes de la comida. Durante el recreo a las diez y veinte, comí una galleta y jugué al baloncesto. Durante la hora de comer, comimos en el comedor y después fui al club de teatro porque es mi pasatiempo favorito. Las clases terminaron a las cuatro y volví a casa para cenar y hacer mis deberes.

Yesterday I went to school by bus and when I arrived I chatted with my friends. Lessons began at 9 and I had 5 classes of 40 minutes each before lunch. During break at 10.20 I ate a biscuit and played basketball. During the lunch hour we ate in the canteen and afterwards I went to drama club because it's my favourite hobby. Lessons finished at 4 and I went home to have dinner and do my homework.

Opinion of homework

Aunque sean útiles para comprender lo que hemos aprendido en el colegio, los deberes me molestan porque los profes nos dan demasiados. Yo tengo dos horas de deberes al día y estoy siempre agotado. Si no los hubiéramos, por lo menos durante la semana, sería mucho mejor.

Although it's useful for understanding what we have learnt in class, homework annoys me because the teachers give us too much. I have two hours of homework per day and I'm always exhausted! If we didn't have any, at least during the week, it would be much better.

What you'd change at school

Si pudiera cambiar algo, cambiaría el uniforme porque es incómodo y feo. Estoy harto de él. También no habría deberes durante la semana. Lo importante es que los estudiantes estén totalmente despiertos en clase para que puedan estudiar y aprender. Seria todavía mejor si las clases empezaran más tarde porque, según los científicos, los jóvenes necesitan más sueño por la mañana.

If I could change something I would change the uniform because it's uncomfortable and ugly. I'm sick of it. Also there wouldn't be any homework during the week. The important thing is that students are wide awake in class so that they can study and learn. It would even better if lessons began later because, according to scientists, young people need more sleep in the morning.

School rules

Las reglas son bastante estrictas. Por ejemplo, no se puede usar el móvil durante las clases; no se puede comer chicle tampoco. Si charlamos, los profes se enfadan. Ayer gané un castigo por hablar en clase y tuve que quedarme en el colegio hasta las cinco de la tarde. El maquillaje está prohibido pero las chicas lo ponen de todas formas.

The rules are quite strict. For example, you can't use your phone during lessons; you can't chew gum either. If we chat, the teachers get cross. Yesterday I got a detention for talking in class and had to stay at school until 5pm. Make-up isn't allowed but the girls wear it anyway.

Ideal school

Mi colegio ideal sería grande y moderno y estaría cerca de mi casa. Habría un polideportivo, donde pasaríamos muchísimas horas jugando al baloncesto, habría una piscina enorme y un cine. No habría uniforme y los profes no darían deberes durante la semana. Las clases empezarían al mediodía porque según los científicos, los jóvenes necesitan más sueño por la mañana. ¡Qué perfecto!

My ideal school would be big and modern and would be near my house. There would be a sports centre where we would spend many hours playing basketball, an enormous pool and a cinema. There wouldn't be a uniform and the teachers wouldn't give homework. Lessons would begin at midday because according to scientists, young people need more sleep in the morning. How perfect!

Primary school

Cuando era joven iba a una escuela primaria cerca de mi casa. Los profes eran simpáticos y no nos daban tantos deberes que ahora. ¡Qué bueno! Había un gran jardín donde solíamos jugar durante el recreo. Lo malo era que no me gustaba la comida escolar porque nos daban demasiadas verduras.

When I was Young I went to a primary school near my house. The teachers were nice and didn't give us as much homework as they do now. How great! There was a big garden where we used to play at breaktime. The bad thing was that I didn't like the school dinners because they gave us too many vegetables.

Spanish and English schools

Parece que los colegios españoles son menos estrictos que los colegios ingleses. No tienen uniforme y el ambiente en el colegio es mucho más agradable porque los alumnos no tienen miedo de los profes. Mi amiga española me dijo que no tiene exámenes cada año como nosotros. ¡Qué suerte! Estoy tan envidioso de los estudiantes españoles. Lo malo es que al fin y al cabo, parece que los estudiantes españoles no tienen tanto éxito como nosotros después del colegio, y el desempleo va aumentando entre los jóvenes españoles.

It seems that Spanish schools are less strict than English schools. They don't have uniform and the atmosphere in the school is much nicer because the pupils are not scared of the teachers. My Spanish friend told me that she doesn't have exams every year like we do. How lucky! I am so jealous of the Spanish students. The bad thing is that at the end of the day, it seems that Spanish students are less successful then us after school and unemployment is rising amongst Spanish young people.

Future education

El año que viene voy a seguir estudiando el inglés, la historia y las matemáticas porque son mis asignaturas favoritas. Dejaré las matemáticas y las ciencias porque me aburren. Trabajaré duro para que pueda ir a una buena universidad, donde espero estudiar el derecho.

Next year I am going to carry on studying English, history and maths because they are my favourite subjects. I will give up maths and science because they bore me. I will work hard so I can go to a good university, where I hope to study law.

Part-time job

El año pasado pasé una semana trabajando en un colegio y me gustó mucho, pero he currado un montón y no gané nada. Ahora tengo un trabajo a tiempo parcial desde hace dos meses en un restaurante en mi barrio que se llama Pizza Mama y es harina de otro costal. Trabajo el sábado de las dos hasta las seis de la tarde. Trabajo en la cocina, lavando los platos y preparando las verduras y las ensaladas. En el restaurante mismo, pongo las mesas y sirvo a los clientes. Lo que más me gusta es el dinero porque los clientes siempre me dan propinas enormes. ¡Me lo paso bomba!

Last year I spent a week working in a school and I liked it a lot but I worked my socks off and earned nothing. Now I have had a part time job for the past two months in a restaurant in my area called Pizza Mama and it's something else entirely. I work on Saturdays from 2 till 6. I work in the kitchen washing dishes and preparing vegetables and salads. In the restaurant itself I lay the tables and serve clients. What I like most is the money because the clients always give huge tips. I love it!

Future job

No sé exactamente qué voy a hacer cuando sea mayor. Lo importante es que sea interesante. Me gustaría hacerme profe de historia porque es mi asignatura favorita y los profes tienen suerte porque no trabajan durante el verano.

I don't know exactly what I want to do when I'm older. The important thing is that it is interesting. I would like to become a history teacher because it's my favourite subject, and teachers are lucky because they don't work during the summer.

Ideal job

Si pudiera elegir, y si no tuviera que ganar dinero, iría a un país del tercero mundo para trabajar como médico voluntario. Hay millones de personas que sufren debido a las guerras y al terrorismo y me gustaría hacer algo para ayudarles.

If I could choose and if I didn't have to earn money I would go to a third world country to do voluntary work as a doctor. There are millions of people suffering because of wars and terrorism and I'd like to do something to help them.

MODERN WORLD AND ENVIRONMENT

Nowadays what are the biggest environmental problems?

Hoy en día, hay un montón de problemas medioambientales. Lo que más me preocupa es la contaminación. Los coches, las fábricas, y la industria emiten gases tóxicos que suben en la atmosfera y causan la contaminación del aire, el calentamiento global y el efecto invernadero. Por consiguiente, las temperaturas aumentan, se funden los casquetes polares y el nivel de los mares va aumentando. Me da miedo por las generaciones futuras debido a los problemas de calentamiento global.

Nowadays, there are lots of environmental problems. What worries me most is pollution. Cars, factories and industry emit toxic gases, which go into the atmosphere and cause air pollution, global warming and the greenhouse effect. Consequently, the temperatures increase, the polar ice caps melt and the sea level rises. I am afraid for the future generations due to the problems of global warming.

Why protect the environment?

A pesar de nuestros esfuerzos, nuestro planeta está a punto de morir. ¡Qué desastre! Si no hacemos nada, la situación solo empeorará, asi que hace falta que todos luchemos por el medioambiente. Es imposible cerrar los ojos ante los problemas asociados con el calentamiento global.

In spite of our efforts, our planet is about to die. What a disaster! If we do not do anything, the situation will only get worse, so we must all fight for the environment. It is impossible to close our eyes to the problems associated with global warming.

Recycling

Creo que la protección del planeta debería ser la responsabilidad de cada uno. Lo más importante es actuar, incluso el acto más sencillo marca la diferencia. En mi familia no dejamos en nuestro empeño de reciclar todo; el cartón, el papel, las botellas, el plástico, el vidrio, las latas y el embalaje.

I believe that the protection of the planet should be everybody's responsibility. The most important thing is to act, even the smallest act can make a difference. In my family we try our best to recycle everything; cardboard, paper, bottles, plastic, glass, tins and packaging.

The importance of recycling

Hoy en día la situación medioambiental es muy preocupada. Es imprescindible que reciclemos todo lo posible para que los recursos naturales no se agoten y para que nuestros hijos puedan vivir en un mundo limpio.

Nowadays the situation in relation to the environment is very worrying. It is essential that we recycle everything possible so our natural resources don't run out and so that our children can have a clean world.

What do you do for the environment at home?

Hago lo que puedo para proteger el medioambiente. Por ejemplo, me ducho en lugar de bañarme para ahorrar agua, apago las luces para ahorrar electricidad, y cierro los grifos cuando no se usan. Además, no dejamos en nuestro empeño de reciclar el cartón, el papel, el plástico y el vidrio. Aprovecho el transporte público en lugar de viajar en coche, y compro productos ecológicos.

I do what I can to protect the environment. For example, I shower instead of taking a bath to save water, I turn off the lights to save electricity and the taps when I'm not using them. Also we do our best to recycle cardboard, paper, plastic and glass. I make the most of public transport instead of travelling by car and I buy green products.

What do you do for the environment at school?

En colegio no dejamos en nuestro empeño de hacer todo lo posible para proteger el medioambiente. Hay una papelera de reciclaje en todas las aulas, apagamos las luces cuando salimos de las aulas para ahorrar electricidad y los profesores nos animan a utilizar el transporte público en lugar de un coche para viajar a colegio, porque el acto más sencillo puede marcar la diferencia.

At school we do our best to do everything possible to protect the environment. There is a recycling bin in every classroom, we turn off the lights when we leave the classrooms to save electricity, and the teachers encourage us to use public transport instead of a car to travel to school, because the simplest act can make a difference.

What should we be doing for the environment?

Es imprescindible que todos luchemos por el medioambiente para que los recursos naturales no se agoten y para que nuestros hijos puedan vivir en un mundo limpio.

Deberíamos seguir haciendo todo lo posible porque el acto más sencillo puede marcar la diferencia. Por ejemplo, deberíamos ducharnos en lugar de bañarnos para ahorrar agua, apagar las luces cuando salimos de un cuarto para ahorrar electricidad, reciclar todo lo posible y aprovechar el transporte público en vez de viajar en coche para reducir la contaminación del aire.

It is essential that we all fight for the environment so that natural resources don't run out and so that our children can live in a clean world. We should continue to do everything possible because the simplest act can make a difference. For example, we should shower instead of having baths to save water, we should turn off the lights when we leave a room to save electricity, recycle everything possible and we should make the most of public transport instead of travelling by car in order to reduce air pollution.

What should the government do for the environment?

Es fundamental que tengamos leyes para proteger el medioambiente. Por ejemplo, opino que el gobierno debería limitar el número de coches en las carreteras y debería construir más rutas para ciclistas para que podamos usar bicicletas en lugar del coche. Si hubiera más rutas para ciclistas pienso que no habría tanta contaminación del aire.

It's fundamental that we have laws to protect the environment. For example, I think that the government should limit the number of cars on the roads and should construct more cycle routes so that we can use bicycles instead of cars. If there were more cycle routes I think that there wouldn't be as much air pollution.

The causes of poverty in the world

Lo que más me preocupa es la pobreza. La mitad del planeta vive en la miseria y la otra mitad tira comida en buen estado. La pobreza se extiende cada vez más, a causa de las guerras, del clima que va cambiando y de conflictos políticos. Las ciudades del mundo están superpobladas, y en poco tiempo habrá grandes problemas de vivienda. Los conflictos mundiales obligan a millones de personas a huir la hambruna y la persecución. Actualmente, la crisis de refugiados en Europa es una situación humanitaria critica. Incluso en Inglaterra, mucha gente vive por debajo del umbral de la pobreza y la situación va empeorando. Hay un montón de familias donde nadie ha tenido un empleo en generaciones. El gobierno debería hacer más para ayudar los niños de estas familias para que puedan acceder a la educación y las oportunidades que merecen.

What worries me most is poverty. Half the world is living in poverty and the other half is throwing away decent food. Poverty is becoming more and more widespread because of wars, a changing climate and political conflict. The cities of the world are overpopulated, and in a short time there will be big problems with living space. World conflicts force millions of people to flee hunger and persecution. Currently the refugee crisis in Europe is a critical humanitarian situation. Even in England lots of people live below the poverty line and the situation is getting worse. There are lots of families where nobody has had a job for generations. The government should do more to encourage the children of these families so that they can access the education and the opportunities they deserve.

Importance of the news

Las noticias pueden tener una gran influencia positiva. Son informativas sobre temas actuales y todos tenemos que saber lo que pasa en el mundo. Sin embargo, lo importante es que las noticias sean imparciales, porque los medios son tan poderosos hoy en día. Es imprescindible que tengamos leyes para que los medios no puedan mentir y manipular sus lectores, como lo hacen en otros países del mundo.

The news can have a major positive influence. It informs us on current issues and we all need to know what is happening in the world. However, what is important is that the news is unbiased because the media is so powerful today. It is essential that we have laws so that the media cannot lie and manipulate its readers as they do in other countries in the world

Do you watch the news?

Las noticias me interesan y si tuviera más tiempo, leería un periódico todos los días, pero los profes nos dan demasiados deberes y me cuesta estar al día. Tengo la aplicación de la BBC en mi móvil que me avisa cuando pasa algo importante en el mundo, y si quiero saber más, hago clic en el icono para abrirlo.

I am interested in the news and if I had more time I would read a paper every day, but the teachers give us too much homework and I find it hard to stay up to date. I have the BBC app on my phone which tells me when something important happens in the world and if I want to know more, I click on the icon to open it.

What's in the news at the moment?

En cuanto a los titulares, a menudo tratan del terrorismo o del medioambiente. Parece que estamos en estado permanente de guerra, y no sabemos cuándo o dónde será el próximo ataque terrorista. Además, los problemas medioambientales van empeorando. Debido al cambio climático hay más terremotos, tormentas e inundaciones que matan a muchísimas personas. También, la situación política en Europa sigue siendo delicada, debido a la subida de sentimientos antiinmigrantes. Mucha gente piensa que la inmigración provoca el terrorismo porque hemos abierto las puertas a todos, incluso los criminales. Pero al mismo tiempo, tenemos que hacer frente a la crisis humanitaria. ¡Qué complicado!

As far as the headlines are concerned, they are often about terrorism or the environment. It seems that we are in a permanent state of war and we don't know when or where the next terrorist attack will be. Moreover, environmental problems are getting worse. Due to climate change there are more earthquakes, storms and floods which kill a lot of people. Also, the political situation in Europe continues to be delicate due to the rise of anti-immigration feeling. Lots of people think that immigration causes terrorism because we have opened the doors to everyone, including criminals. But at the same time we need to face the humanitarian crisis. How complex!

Do you watch TV?

Si, veo las telenovelas todos los días para relajarme, y porque me hacen reír y los vemos juntos, mis hermanos y yo. Además, nunca me pierdo los programas de deportes, especialmente los partidos de futbol. Veo las noticias de vez en cuando porque me informan y me interesan mucho. Si tuviera más tiempo vería más programas, pero los profes nos dan demasiados deberes.

Yes, I watch soap operas every day to relax and because they make me laugh and I watch them together with my brothers. In addition, I never miss sports programmes, especially football matches. I watch the news from time to time because it is informative and interesting. If I had more time I would watch more programmes but the teachers give us too much homework.

Young people and TV

Creo que si vemos la televisión corremos el riesgo de pasar demasiadas horas encerrados en casa. Puede crear adicción en algunas personas que pierden el control de las horas que pasan delante de la pequeña pantalla y por consiguiente pierden la capacidad de comunicar cara a cara. Sin embargo, pienso que ver la televisión es mejor que los videojuegos y las redes sociales porque los documentales pueden ser una herramienta educativa ya que permiten que los jóvenes sean conscientes de problemas sociales y globales.

I believe that if we watch television we risk spending too much time stuck at home. It can create addiction in some people who lose control of the hours that they spend in front of the small screen and consequently lose the capacity to communicate face to face. However, I think that watching television is better than video games and social networks because documentaries can be an educational tool as they make young people aware of social and global problems.

Advantages of TV

Para empezar, la televisión puede ser una herramienta educativa dado que hay muchos programas que ayudan a los niños a aprender. Por ejemplo, los documentales tienen una influencia positiva puesto que no solo nos divierten, sino también nos enseñan. Además, la televisión puede ser una diversión inocua y puede ayudar a la gente a descansar y desconectar de la rutina diaria. Opino que la televisión es un buen medio de relajarse después de un día estresante en el colegio.

Firstly, television can be an educational tool because there are many programmes which help children to learn. For example, documentaries have a positive influence because not only do they entertain us but also teach us. In addition, television can be a harmless hobby and can help people to rest and disconnect from their daily routine. I think that television is a good way to relax after a stressful day at school.

Disadvantages of TV

Creo que si vemos la televisión corremos el riesgo de pasar demasiadas horas encerrados en casa. Puede crear adicción en algunas personas que pierden el control de las horas que pasan delante de la pequeña pantalla y por consiguiente pierden la capacidad de comunicar cara a cara. Además, según mucha gente, hay cada vez más violencia en la televisión, particularmente en los dibujos animados que están dirigidos a los niños. ¡Qué horror! Los espectadores de las pelis de acción se están insensibilizando a la violencia y hoy en día los jóvenes ya no están impactados por imágenes chocantes.

I believe that if we watch television we risk spending too much time stuck at home. It can create addiction in some people who lose control of the hours that they spend in front of the small screen and consequently lose the capacity to communicate face to face. Also, according to many people, there is more and more violence on television, particularly in cartoons, which are aimed at children. How awful! People who watch action films are becoming desensitized to violence and young people are no longer affected by shocking images.

Advertising

Hoy en día podemos ver y oír la publicidad en todas partes. Vaya donde vaya, hay carteles o anuncios publicitarios, viajando en el automóvil vemos vallas publicitarias en las calles y a la vez escuchamos en la radio avisos publicitaros. Al leer un periódico o una revista encontramos anuncios publicitarios y mientras navegamos por Internet observamos anuncios por todas partes.

Nowadays we can see and hear advertising everywhere. Wherever you go there are signs or adverts, travelling by car we can see billboards in the streets and at the same time listen to adverts on the radio. When reading a newspaper or magazine we find adverts and while we surf the Internet we see adverts everywhere.

Positives of advertising

La principal ventaja de la publicidad es promover y dar a conocer al público un producto, e informar al consumidor sobre los beneficios que presenta el producto. Es la manera más efectiva de aumentar el número de ventas de un producto, sobre todo hoy en día mediante las redes sociales. Además, aunque pueda ser molesto, la publicidad es la razón por la cual las redes sociales como Facebook permanecen gratis.

The main advantage of advertising is to promote and publicise a product to the public, and to inform the consumer about the benefits of the product. It is the most effective method of increasing the sales of a product, especially today by using social networks. Also, althought it can be annoying, advertising is the reason why social networks like Facebook remain free of charge.

Negatives of advertising

La publicidad a muchas veces nos engaña para que compremos productos o servicios, y puede provocar la avidez. Los anuncios que promueven la comida basura y los cigarrillos deberían ser prohibidos porque promueven productos que son malos para la salud y pueden causar enfermedades graves como el cáncer. Además, la publicidad puede tener una influencia peligrosa en los jóvenes que piensan que deberían ser tan delgados y tan guapos como los modelos que ven en los anuncios, en la tele, donde sea. La presión puede causar trastornos alimentarios como anorexia.

Advertising often deceives us to make us buy products or services and can provoke greed in people. I think that adverts promoting junk food and cigarettes should be banned because they promote products which are bad for your health and can cause serious illnesses like cancer. Also, advertising can have a dangerous influence on young people who think they should be as thin and gorgeous as the models they see on the adverts, on TV, wherever. The pressure can cause eating disorders like anorexia.

Cinema

Me gustan las películas y el cine. Los domingos por la mañana, aunque tenga poco dinero, voy al cine y mi hermana mayor me acompaña. Antes de ir, busco las mejores películas en internet. A mi hermana le gustan las películas de amor mientras que yo prefiero las películas de ciencia ficción y de acción. Si tuviera más dinero iría todos los días, pero cuesta un ojo de la cara y no puedo permitírmelo.

I like films and cinema. On Sunday mornings, although I don't have much money, I go to the cinema with my older sister. Before going I find the best films on the Internet. My sister likes romantic films whilst I prefer science fiction and action films. If I had more money, I'd go every day but it costs an arm and a leg and I can't afford it.

What films do you like?

En cuanto al cine, no me gustan nada las películas románticas. Prefiero las películas de acción, sobre todo las pelis de James Bond porque son emocionantes y no me aburren. Hay un montón de efectos especiales y juegan muchísimas estrellas de cine. Suelo ir al cine todos los fines de semana con mis amigos. Si tuviera más dinero iría todos los días, pero cuesta un ojo de la cara y no puedo permitírmelo.

As for cinema, I do not like romantic films at all. I prefer action films, above all James Bond films because they are exciting and they don't bore me. There are loads of special effects and lots of movie stars acting in them. I usually go to the cinema every weekend with my friends. If I had more money, I'd go every day but it costs an arm and a leg and I can't afford it.

Cinema or TV?

Prefiero el cine porque a mí me encantan las pelis de ciencia ficción y prefiero verlas en la pantalla grande. Disfruto mucho más de los efectos especiales, de la banda sonora y de los efectos visuales. Además, cuando ves una película en casa, hay un montón de distracciones, y siempre hay alguien que quiere cambiar de canal.

I prefer the cinema because I love science fiction films and I prefer to watch them on the big screen. I enjoy the effects, the soundtrack and the visual effects much more. Also when you watch a film at home there are loads of distractions and there is always someone who wants to change channel.

The last film you saw

Acabo de ver Titanic y fue estupendo. Trata de dos jóvenes amantes que cruzan sus destinos en el viaje inaugural del crucero Titanic. Pero cuando el crucero choca contra un iceberg en el gélido Océano Atlántico Norte, su apasionado encuentro amoroso se convierte en una desesperada carrera por sobrevivir. No me sorprende que es la película de más éxito de todos los tiempos.

I have just watched Titanic and it was great. It is about two young lovers whose destinies cross on the inaugural journey of the cruise ship Titanic. But when the ship hits an iceberg in the frozen North Atlantic their passionate encounter becomes a desperate race to survive. It doesn't surprise me that it's the most successful film of all time.

Mobile phones – do you have one and why?

Tengo suerte porque tengo mi propio móvil desde hace cinco años y lo uso para mandar mensajes, hablar con mis amigos en las redes sociales, escuchar música, sacar fotos y navegar por internet. Lo que más me gusta es que los móviles hacen la comunicación más sencilla, pero si tuviera más dinero, compraría el ultima modelo porque mi móvil es fuera de moda. No puedo prescindir del móvil. Soy adicto.

I am lucky because I have had my own mobile for 5 years and I use it to send messages, talk to my friends on social networks, listen to music, take photos and go on the internet. What I like most is that mobiles make communication much easier but if I had more money, I would buy the latest model because my mobile is out-dated. I could not survive without my phone. I am addicted to it.

Young people and mobile phones

A los jóvenes les gustan los móviles porque son extremadamente útiles, para chatear con amigos en las redes sociales, descargar y escuchar música, sacar fotos y navegar por la red. Muchas jóvenes no podrían prescindir del móvil y su adicción puede ser peligroso.

Young people like mobile phones because they are extremely useful, to chat to friends on social networks, download and listen to music, take photos and surf the web. Most young people couldn't manage without a mobile and their addiction can be dangerous.

Advantages of technology

1. No cabe duda de que los móviles y el internet hacen la comunicación mucho más sencilla. La mayor ventaja es que se puede comunicar con personas de todas partes del mundo.
2. Podemos informarnos sobre cualquier cosa cuando queramos. Me ayuda con mis deberes.

3. La tecnología deja que yo este siempre en contacto con todos y aprovecho las aplicaciones como Whatsapp y Snapchat para comunicar con mis amigos todo el tiempo.
4. Me pongo al día con las aplicaciones de noticias, que me avisan cuando pasa algo importante.
5. Se puede descargar películas y música. Suelo pasar mucho tiempo escuchando música en mi móvil y hace el viaje al colegio mucho más divertido. ¡Qué suerte tenemos! No hay límites.

1. *There is no doubt that mobile phones make communication much easier. The main advantage is that you can communicate with people all over the world*
2. *We can find out about anything whenever we like. It helps me with my homework.*
3. *Technology allows me to stay in contact with everyone and I make the most of apps like Whatsapp and Snapchat to communicate with my friends all the time.*
4. *I stay up to date using the news apps which let me know when something important happens*
5. *You can download films and music. I usually spend a lot of time listening to music on my phone and it makes the journey to school much more fun. How lucky we are! There are no limits.*

Disadvantages of technology

1. Lo que más me preocupa es que hoy en día los jóvenes se quedan pegados a sus aparatos y puede ponerse adictos. Pierden la capacidad de comunicar cara a cara y resulta que los estudiantes se esfuercen menos en hacer sus tareas porque están distraídos y se vuelven solitarios y tristes.
2. Nos estamos poniendo tan adictos a nuestros aparatos que corremos el riesgo de tener accidentes cuando conducimos o cruzamos la calle.
3. Además, si mandas un mensaje electrónico, esperas una respuesta inmediata y eso puede provocar el estrés y otros problemas de salud.
4. Siempre hay riesgos de virus y la información privada puede ser mal utilizada y corremos el riesgo de ser víctimas de delito informático.
5. Otro riesgo del uso de Internet es estar en contacto con desconocidos, especialmente para los jóvenes. Personas peligrosas pueden ocultarse detrás de la pantalla y usar identidades falsas para que no sepamos quién nos habla en realidad. Por ejemplo, ayer vi las noticias y hablaron sobre una chica de dieciséis años quien conoció a su 'novio' a través Facebook, pero en realidad era un hombre viejo y desafortunadamente la mató. ¡Qué chocante!

1. *What worries me most is that nowadays, young people stay glued to their devices and you can become addicted. They lose the capacity to communicate face to face and the result is that students strive less to do their homework because they are distracted and they become lonely and sad.*
2. *We are getting so addicted to our devices that we risk having accidents when we are driving or crossing the road.*
3. *In addition, if you send a message electronically, you expect an immediate answer so that pressure can cause stress and other health problems.*
4. *There are always risks of viruses infecting our computers and private information can be misused and we risk being victims of cybercrime.*
5. *Another risk of Internet use is being in contact with strangers, especially for young people. Dangerous people can hide behind the screen and use false identities so that we don't know who we are really speaking too. For example, yesterday I saw the news and they spoke about a 16 year old girl who met her 'boyfriend' on Facebook, but in reality he was an old man and unfortunately he killed her. How shocking!*

The future of mobile phones

En el futuro, creo que los móviles se volverán más flacos con pantallas más grandes y más útiles. Pero pase lo que pase serán más poderosos y tendremos que tener cuidado con la información que compartimos por internet porque corremos el riesgo de ser víctimas de delito informático.

In the future, I believe that mobiles with become thinner with bigger screens and more useful. But whatever happens they will be more powerful and we will have to be careful with the information we share on the internet because we risk being victims of cybercrime.

SOCIAL ACTIVITIES, FITNESS AND HEALTH

What do you eat on a normal day?

Cada mañana desayuno cereales porque son una fuente de energía y esto me ayuda cuando trabajo. Como un bocadillo y fruta al colegio, pero si tuviera la oportunidad me gustaría comer pescado frito con patatas fritas. Al volver a casa, siempre como chocolate, aunque sea malo para la salud, porque soy adicta y se me hace agua la boca. Ceno carne y verduras, pasta, pollo o pizza. Debería comer menos chocolate y más fruta y verduras para evitar enfermedades cardiacas.

Every morning I eat cereal because it is a source of energy and this helps me when I work. I eat a sandwich and fruit at school but if I had the chance I would like to eat fish and chips. On returning home, I always eat chocolate although it is bad for you, because I am addicted and it makes my mouth water. I eat meat and vegetables, pasta, chicken or pizza for dinner. I should eat less chocolate and more fruit and vegetables in order to avoid heart problems.

General eating habits

Intento comer de manera sana, aunque sea bastante difícil de vez en cuando. Como cinco porciones de frutas y verduras al día, y evito el azúcar. Me cuesta a veces porque me encanta comer chocolate y dulces, pero opino que se puede tomar los alimentos no saludables en moderación. Cuando era joven odiaba la comida sana y cada día pedía la comida rápida. Mi comida favorita era patatas fritas y no quería comer nada más.

I try to eat healthily although it is quite difficult sometimes. I eat 5 portions of fruit and vegetables per day and I avoid sugar. It's hard sometimes because I love eating chocolate and sweet things but I think it's okay to have unhealthy things in moderation. When I was young I used to hate healthy food and every day I asked for fast food. My favourite food was chips and I didn't want to eat anything else.

What don't you like eating

Suelo comer todo, pero si tuviera elegir un tipo de comida que no me gusta mucho, sería el espárrago.

I usually eat everything, but if I had to choose a type of food that I don't like very much, it would be asparagus.

Lunch at school

Almuerzo en la cantina donde suelo tomar un bocadillo de pollo o una ensalada. Afortunadamente la comida escolar ha mejorado a lo largo de los años, tanto en cuanto a sabor como a nutrición. ¡Qué suerte tenemos! Ayer comí pasta con champiñones. Fue delicioso.

I eat lunch in the canteen where I usually have a chicken sandwich or a salad. Fortunately, school lunches have improved throughout the years, in flavour and in nutrition. How lucky we are!

Favourite food

Mi comida favorita es el chocolate, aunque sea malo para la salud, porque es delicioso y se me hace agua la boca. Como chocolate todos los días, después del colegio para que tenga la energía que necesito para hacer mis deberes.

My favourite food is chocolate although it is bad for my health because it is delicious and makes my mouth water. I eat chocolate every day after school so that I have the energy I need to do my homework.

How to stay healthy

Para llevar una vida sana se debe comer una dieta variada con cinco porciones de fruta o verduras al día, ya que nos dan vitaminas importantes. Deberíamos evitar la comida basura porque contiene demasiado azúcar y grasa y provoca la obesidad. Además, es importante hacer deporte, evitar el alcohol y no fumar, porque puede causar enfermedades graves. Sin embargo, opino que se puede tomar los alimentos no saludables en moderación.

In order to lead a healthy life, we must eat a varied diet with five portions of fruit and vegetables a day because they give us important vitamins. We should avoid junk food because it contains too much sugar and fat and causes obesity. In addition, it is important to do sport, avoid alcohol and not smoke because it can cause serious illnesses. However, I think that you can eat unhealthy food in moderation.

How you stay healthy

Para mantener la forma hago deporte por lo menos tres veces a la semana al aire libre, bebo dos litros de agua al día y tomo cinco porciones de fruta o verduras. Nunca fumo y nunca he probado una droga. Siempre intento evitar la comida basura y materia grasa, aunque sea difícil porque no puedo prescindir del chocolate, e intento dormir ocho horas como mínimo cada noche.

In order to keep in shape, I do sport at least three times a week in the fresh air, I drink two litres of water a day and I have 5 portions of fruit or vegetables. I never smoke and I have never taken drugs. I always try to avoid junk and fatty foods, although it is difficult because I can't manage without chocolate, and I try to sleep eight hours minimum every night.

Do you like sport?

Sí, me gusta muchísimo el deporte. Es mi asignatura favorita en el colegio porque es fácil y el profesor es divertido. Lo que me gusta más es estar al aire libre. Después de una hora de tenis me siento muy relajado. Suelo jugar al tenis tres veces a la semana, y los sábados me encanta aprovechar el buen tiempo y hacer ciclismo con mi padre. Cuando sea mayor, voy a seguir haciendo deporte para mantener la forma y un buen estado de ánimo.

Yes, I like sport a lot. It is my favourite subject at school because it is easy and the teacher is fun. What I like the most is being in the fresh air. After an hour of tennis I feel very relaxed. I usually play tennis three times a week and on Saturdays I love to make the most of the good weather and go cycling with my father. When I grow up I'm going to carry on doing sport to keep fit and stay happy.

Why should we do sport?

Deberíamos hacer deporte ya que es genial para mejorar el estado de ánimo, reducir el estrés y mantenerse en forma. Se puede también hacer nuevos amigos y aumentar la auto-confianza. Si no hiciéramos deporte, correríamos el riesgo de engordar, y la obesidad puede provocar enfermedades graves.

We should do sport because it is a great way to improve the mood, reduce stress and keep fit. You can also make new friends and improve your self-confidence. If we didn't do sport, we would risk getting fat and obesity can cause serious illnesses.

Todays' health problems

Hay un montón de problemas de salud en mi país, pero lo que más me preocupa es la obesidad. Se dice que casi la mitad de los niños británicos son obesos. Pasan demasiado tiempo delante de la televisión o pegados a sus móviles y no hacen ejercicio. También suelen comer la comida basura porque es barata, sabrosa y fácil a obtener. Contiene mucha grasa, sal y azúcar y eso puede provocar enfermedades como la cardiopatía.

There are loads of health problems in my country. What worries me most is obesity. It is said that almost half of British children are obese. They spend too much time in front of the television or glued to their mobiles and don't exercise. Also they eat junk food because it is cheap, tasty and easy to get. It contains lots of fat, salt and sugar and this can cause illness like heart disease.

The solution to health problems

Es imprescindible que hagamos algo para mejorar la situación. Si fuera ministro de deporte, lanzaría una campaña para enseñar a los niños sobre los beneficios del deporte. Sería genial si hubiera unas personas famosas a las que los jóvenes admiran que podrían motivarles a cambiar su estilo de vida. También, es esencial que haya polideportivos en todos partes para que los jóvenes puedan acceder al deporte fácilmente. Ya existen, pero tienes que ser miembro y es caro, asi que los jóvenes no pueden permitírselo. Además la comida sana debería ser más barata

It is necessary that we do something to improve the situation. If I were minister of sport I would launch a campaign to teach children about the benefits of sport. It would be great if there were some celebrities who young people admired that could motivate them to change their lifestyle. Also, it is essential that there are sports centres everywhere so that young people can access sport easily. They already exist but you have to be a member and it is expensive, therefore young people can't afford it. In addition, healthy food should be cheaper.

Sickness

Tengo suerte porque estoy mal casi nunca. Normalmente si no es serio, hay que guardar cama, pero si no se siente mejor después de algunos días, tiene que ir al médico. Se puede evitar enfermedades llevando un estilo de vida sano.

I am lucky because I am almost never sick. Normally, if it is not serious you have to stay in bed but if you do not feel better after a few days, you have to go to the doctor. We can avoid illnesses by living a healthy lifestyle.

Smoking

A mi parecer, fumar es absurdo porque todo el mundo sabe que causa enfermedades graves como el cáncer y la bronquitis crónica. Nunca fumaré. Pienso que los jóvenes de hoy en día fuman por un montón de razones, pero lo más importante es la presión del grupo. Si vas a una fiesta y hay muchas personas que están fumando, hay la tentación de hacer lo mismo para sentirse parte del grupo.

In my opinion, smoking is ridiculous because everyone knows that it causes serious illnesses like cancer and chronic bronchitis. I will never smoke. I think that young people today smoke for loads of reasons, but the most important is peer pressure. If you go to a party and there are lots of people smoking, there is the temptation to do the same to feel part of the group.

Alcohol

A mi parecer, el consumo excesivo de alcohol es absurdo porque todo el mundo sabe que causa enfermedades graves como la cirrosis hepática y el cáncer. Nunca beberé de manera excesiva. Pienso que los jóvenes de hoy en día beben alcohol por un montón de razones, pero lo más importante es la presión del grupo. Les falta la auto-confianza y recurren al alcohol para sentirse más valientes. Si vas a una fiesta y hay muchas personas que están borrachas, hay la tentación de hacer lo mismo.

In my opinion, the excessive consumption of alcohol is ridiculous because everyone knows that it causes serious illnesses like cirrhosis of the liver and cancer. I will never drink excessively. I think that young people today drink alcohol for loads of reasons, but the most important is peer pressure. They lack self-confidence and turn to alcohol to feel braver. If you go to a party and there are lots of drunk people, there is the temptation to do the same.

Drugs

A mi parecer, tomar drogas es absurdo porque todo el mundo sabe que causan enfermedades graves como ataques de pánico y pueden alterar la manera cómo funciona el cerebro. Nunca tomaré drogas. Pienso que los jóvenes de hoy en día toman drogas por un montón de razones, pero lo más importante es la presión del grupo. Les falta la auto-confianza y recurren a las drogas para sentirse más valientes. Si vas a una fiesta y hay muchas personas que están tomando drogas, hay la tentación de hacer lo mismo para sentirse parte del grupo.

In my opinion, taking drugs is ridiculous because everyone knows that they cause serious illnesses like panic attacks and can alter brain function. I will never take drugs. I think that young people today take drugs for loads of reasons, but the most important is peer pressure. They lack self-confidence and turn to drugs to feel braver. If you go to a party and there are lots of people taking drugs, there is the temptation to do the same.

Vegetarianism

Hay un montón de razones por el vegetarianismo. No solo es que no quieren matar a los animales sino también tienen razones relacionadas con la salud y el medioambiente. Algunos dicen que comer carne en exceso es malo para la salud y además la producción de carne destruye las selvas tropicales y el medioambiente.

There are many reasons for vegetarianism. Not only do they not want to kill animals but also they have reasons in relation to health and the environment. Some say that eating meat excessively is bad for your health and in addition the production of meat destroys tropical forests and the environment.

Hobbies when you were young

Cuando era joven hacía un poco menos deporte, pero pasaba la mayoría del tiempo en el parque cerca de mi casa, jugando con mis amigos, así que mantenía la forma sin esforzarme. También, veía la tele todos los días y jugaba los videojuegos. Solía leer mucho también.

When I was young I did slightly less sport but I spent the majority of my time in the park near my house, playing with friends so I kept in shape without making an effort. Also, I watched the television every day and played videogames. I used to read a lot as well.

Ideal weekend

Mi fin de semana ideal sería con mi familia y mis amigos. Si pudiera elegir, iría a Londres para ver un espectáculo con mi madre y al volver a mi casa comeríamos pizza. Si fuera posible pasaríamos el día siguiente haciendo natación y jugando a las cartas. ¡Que relajante!

My ideal weekend would be with my family and my friends. If I could choose, I would go to London to watch a show with my mum and on returning home we would eat pizza. If it was possible we would spend the following day swimming and playing cards. How relaxing!

Books you've read

Cuando termino mis deberes, siempre tengo ganas de leer, porque me ayuda a descansar. Sin duda, mi libro favorito es "Harry Potter and the Philosopher's Stone", que acabo de leer por segunda vez. Trata de la escuela Hogwarts de Magia y Hechicería donde Harry conoce a otros niños que tienen poderes especiales y aprende todo lo necesario para ser mago. Para mí lo más importante de leer es poder escaparse del estrés de la vida real.

When I finish my homework, I always want to read because it helps me to relax. Without a doubt my favourite book is "Harry Potter and the Philosopher's Stone" which I have just read for the second time. It is about Hogwarts school of Witchcraft and Wizardry where Harry gets to know other children who have special powers and learns everything necessary to be a wizard. For me the important thing about reading is to escape the stress of real life.

Music and musicians

No toco un instrumento, pero me apasiona la música. Primero me chifla la música electrónica porque es animada y energética. Cuando voy al gimnasio, la escucho para que pueda correr más rápidamente. También la música me ayuda a descansar, por ejemplo, después de un día estresante al colegio lo que más me gusta es escuchar mi artista favorito, Ed Sheeran. Tengo ganas de verlo en concierto, pero las entradas cuestan un ojo de la cara, y primero tengo que hacer mis quehaceres para que pueda permitírmelo.

I do not play an instrument but I love music. Firstly, I like electronic music because it's animated and energetic. What I go to the gym I listen to it so that I can run faster. Also music helps me to relax, for example after a stressful day at school what I like the most is to listen to favourite artist, Ed Sheeran. I want to see him live but first I have to do my chores so that I can afford it.

Pocket money and shopping

Tengo suerte porque mis padres me dan treinta libras al mes. Normalmente suelo comprar revistas y caramelos, pero el fin de semana pasado lo gasté en ir al cine con mis amigos. Si tuviera la oportunidad, me gustaría recibir más dinero para que pueda comprar más videojuegos, pero mis padres creen que recibo suficiente dinero. ¡Qué pesadilla! No creo que tengan razón.

I am lucky because my parents give me thirty pounds a month. Normally, I buy magazines or videogames, but last weekend I spent it on going to the cinema with my friends. If I had the chance, I would like more money so that I can buy more sweets but I my parents think that I receive enough money. What a nightmare! I don't think they are right.

GLOSSARY OF IMPRESSIVE PHRASES

To be used to spice up your writing AS WELL AS your oral!

USE ALL THE VERB TENSES

Make sure you have used:

- **Present** (including irregulars and reflexives) to describe what you normally do

  Voy al cine / Hago mis deberes

  I go to the cinema / I do my homework

  AND with desde hace ← vivo aquí desde hace cinco años

  I have lived here for 5 years

- **Present continuous** to describe what is currently happening

  Estoy leyendo un libro

  I am reading a book

- **Perfect** to describe what you have done

  He visto muchas películas, pero la mejor fue ...

  I have seen a lot of films but the best one was .....

- **Preterite** to describe events in the past

  Saqué fotos / Tomé el sol

  I took photos / I sunbathed

  AND irregular preterites to show you know them

  Tuve un accidente / Fui al mercado / Puse la mesa

  I had an accident / I went to the market / I laid the table

- **Imperfect** to describe repeated actions in the past

  Vivía en el campo / Solía ver la tele todos los días

  I lived in the countryside / I used to watch TV every day

- **Both types of future** tense

  Voy a ir de vacaciones / Haré mis deberes

  I am going to go on holiday / I will do my homework

- **Conditional** to describe what would happen if certain conditions were fulfilled

  Me gustaría vivir en el campo / Viviría en una casa enorme

  I would like to live in the countryside / I would live in an enormous house

- **Pluperfect** to describe what had happened before the action you are describing

  Cuando volvimos, el perro había comido el pastel

  When we returned, the dog had eaten the cake

- **Present subjunctive** with specific phrases

  ¡Ojalá tengamos éxito! / Trabajo para que pueda ir a una buena universidad

  Hopefully we shall succeed / I work so that I can go to a good university

  AND to talk about the future – cuando sea mayor voy a hacerme profe

  When I'm older I'm going to be a teacher

- **Imperfect subjunctive with the conditional** in "if" sentences

  Si pudiera, cambiaría el uniforme / Si fuera rica, compraría una casa en España

  If I could I would change the uniform / If I was rich I would buy a house in Spain

- **Pluperfect subjunctive with the past conditional** in complex "if" sentences (not required, but impressive!)

  Si hubiera podido, habria hecho mucho más

  If I had been able to, I would have done much more

VERBS THAT TAKE GERUNDS

- Voy a **seguir** estudiando

  I'm going to carry on studying

- **Paso** mucho tiempo trabajando

  I spend a lot of time working

- La situación **va** empeorando

  The situation is getting worse

- **Voy** al colegio andando

  I walk to school

INTERESTING SPANISH VERB USAGE

Aprovechar – to make the most of

aprovecho el buen tiempo para tomar el sol

I make the most of the good weather to sunbathe

Disfrutar (de) – to enjoy – very flexible with or without the de!

Siempre he disfrutado de buena salud

I have always enjoyed good health

Disfruto el buen tiempo

I enjoy the good weather

Where we use get or go + adjective they often have their own verb

Adelgazar	to get thin
Cansarse	to get tired
Emocionarse	to get excited
Enfadarse	to get angry
Enfermarse	to get sick
Engordar	to get fat
Enrojecer	to go red

OTHER VERB STRUCTURES

Después de / antes de comer	before / after eating
Estar a punto de comer	I am about to eat
Acabo de hacer	have just eaten
Al llegar	on arriving

OPINIONS

Pienso que / Creo que / En mi opinión ......porque

Positive opinions

Vale la pena	it's worth it
Me pone feliz	it makes me happy
Me hace reir	it makes me laugh
Tengo ganas de ir de vacaciones	I feel like going on holiday
Espero con ganas	I'm looking forward to
Tengo suerte	I am lucky
Lo que más me gusta es que	what I like most is
Tengo buenas notas	I get good marks
Me lo pasé bomba	I had a great time
No puedo prescindir de él	I can't manage without it
¡Qué bueno!	How brilliant
El mejor país del mundo	the best country in the world

Negative opinions

Lo que no me gusta es que	what I don't like is that
Lo que más me preocupa es que	what worries me most is that
Estoy harto	I'm sick of it
¡Qué pesadilla!	What a nightmare
¡Qué horror!	How horrible!

TENGO EXPRESSIONS

Tengo suerte	I'm lucky
Tengo ganas de	I feel like
Tengo frio / calor	I'm cold / hot
Tengo que	I have to
Tengo hambre / sed	I'm hungry / thirsty
Tengo quince años	I'm 15
Tengo razón	I'm right
Tengo miedo	I am afraid
Tengo prisa	I'm in a hurry

COMPARATIVES AND SUPERLATIVES

Más grande que él	bigger than him
Menos divertido que ella	less fun than her
El mejor del mundo	the best in the world
Es tan deportista como yo	he is as sporty as me

DESDE HACE and HACE

Vivo aquí desde hace cinco años	I have been living here 5 years
Hace dos años fui a España	Two years ago I went to Spain

PRECEDING DIRECT AND INDIRECT OBJECT PRONOUNS

Los profes nos dan muchos deberes	The teachers give us lots of homework
Les encanta la música	I love music
Le regalé un libro	I gave him a book
No me importa	It doesn't matter to me
Lo hago yo	I do it

SUBJUNCTIVE EXPRESSIONS

Si tuviera mucho dinero	If I had a lot of money
Si fuera rico	If I was rich
Si hubiera mas rutas para ciclistas	If there were more cycle paths
Si hubiera tenido el tiempo	If I had had the time
Para que pueda	so that I can
Aunque sea	although it is
No pienso que sea	I don't think it is
¡Ojalá pudiera!	If only I could

PARA, SIN + infinitive

Fui al parque para jugar al tenis	I went to the park to play tennis
Los jóvenes toman drogas sin pensar en las consecuencias	Young people take drugs without thinking about the consequences

IMPERSONAL EXPRESSIONS

Se puede	you can (one can)
Se debe / hay que	you must (one must)

PRONOUNS ATTACHED TO THE INFINITIVE OR GERUND

No puedo permitírmelo	I can't afford it
Para que pueda aprovecharlo	So I can make the most of it
Me gustaría verlo en concierto	I would like to see him in concert

MODALS IN ALL TENSES

No puedo prescindir de mi móvil	I can't do without my mobile
Deberíamos ahorrar agua	We should save water
Podría hacer más ejercicio	I could do more exercise
Solía ver la tele	I used to watch TV
Me gustaría aprender el español	I would like to learn Spanish

SPANISH IDIOMS

Estoy un poco fastidiado	I'm not feeling very well
Tengo el pie fastidiado	I've hurt my foot
Siempre está aprovechando de mi	He is always taking advantage of me
¡Estoy machacado / agotado!	I'm exhausted!
He currado un montón esta semana	I've worked really hard this week!
Voy a pegarme un madrugón	I'm going to get up really early
Él es muy madrugador	He's a really early riser
Llueve a mares	It's pouring with rain
Cuesta un ojo de la cara	It costs an arm and a leg
Se me hace agua la boca	It makes my mouth wáter
Tiene un humor de perros	She is in a bad mood
Gastarse un riñon	to pay through the nose
Harina de otro costal	another thing entirely
Domrir como un tronco	to sleep like a log

Thank you for purchasing this book. I hope it has been useful to you. If you have any questions or comments, please do get in touch via my website www.lucymartintuition.co.uk

If you have found the book useful, please leave us a review on Amazon, and don't forget you can also buy the first book in this series, *How To Ace your French Oral*.

Made in the USA
Charleston, SC
27 September 2016